Original title:
Sapling Songs

Copyright © 2025 Creative Arts Management OÜ
All rights reserved.

Author: Jude Lancaster
ISBN HARDBACK: 978-1-80567-364-4
ISBN PAPERBACK: 978-1-80567-663-8

The Symphony of Young Timber

In the forest where giggles grow,
Young trees sway in a lively show.
They dance with the breeze, so bold and spry,
Chasing squirrels who dart by.

Leaves are clapping, branches cheer,
Whispers of laughter we hold dear.
They tickle the clouds with a playful jest,
Echoing joy, they never rest.

Embracing the Dawn of Life

Morning sun, with a wink so bright,
Sprouts peek out, ready for flight.
They stretch their arms to the golden hue,
As critters giggle, they join the view.

Tiny buds, in a playful race,
Compete to bloom with the sun's embrace.
Each new petal is a silly fling,
A quirky waltz that nature brings.

Echoing the Spirit of Renewal

From soil's depth, a tiny shout,
With roots so ticklish, there's no doubt.
They poke their heads out to join the fun,
Ready to play 'til the day is done.

A chorus of sprouts in vibrant glee,
Insisting that life is plant's decree.
Chortles of buds in a sunny spree,
Celebrating growth, wild and free.

Cadence from the Heart of Nature

Under a giggling moonlit sky,
New leaves jive as stars wink by.
They tell the tales of the night so bright,
With the moon as their stage, it's pure delight.

The breeze hums tunes of a joyful past,
While roots make puns that seem to last.
Nature's rhythm, a whimsical beat,
Leaves tapping along, oh what a treat!

Echoes of Gentle Roots

In the garden where giggles grow,
The daisies dance, putting on a show.
Roots tickle the soil, making it laugh,
As worms hold a party in the green path.

Sunbeams flicker like fireflies bright,
While grasshoppers sing into the night.
A beetle in boots does a tap dance,
He claims it's the start of the great insect prance.

The Green Awakening

A cabbage once dreamed of fame and cheer,
But found it was just too hard to steer.
With lettuce friends, they plotted and planned,
To throw the greatest salad in the land!

Tomatoes giggle, they're blushing red,
While cucumbers joke, 'We're so cool, we're spread!'
Carrots wear sunglasses, feeling quite fly,
As radishes shout, 'Let's reach for the sky!'

Tender Notes from the Earth

The daisies hum a whimsical tune,
While the bumblebees buzz in high afternoon.
A cherry tree chuckles, swaying in glee,
As squirrels play chess in its branches, you see!

With every raindrop, there's laughter and cheer,
The puddles reflect smiles, oh dear!
Frogs jump in rhythm, holding their bets,
As slugs slip and slide, the best of the sets!

Melodies of the Budding World

The flowers hold microphones, ready to sing,
While the wind plays the flute—what a funny thing!
A daffodil jokes, 'I'm brighter than you!'
And the tulips chime in, 'Well, look who's not blue!'

Bees gossip over pollen, buzzing with glee,
Saying, 'Have you heard? The pollen's for free!'
In the patch, every plant shares a rhyme,
Turning the garden into a comedy clime!

Bright Dreams in the Canopy

In the village of leaves, they tell tales,
Of critters in pajamas and wind-blown sails.
A squirrel named Vern, with his silly cap,
Danced with a breeze, then took a nap!

The sun tickled branches, laughed in delight,
While shadows played hide and seek every night.
A rabbit brought cupcakes, oh what a treat!
Now everyone's bouncing, tapping their feet!

The daffodils giggled, swaying with glee,
As ants held a concert, not quite in key.
The moon borrowed cheese from a nearby cow,
To share with the owls who were singing "Meow!"

So if you're out wandering, do stop and stay,
There's humor in nature, come join the play.
Bright dreams are blooming where giggles abound,
In a canopy world where joy can be found.

Journey of the Persisting Stem

Once a tiny twig, with dreams to ascend,
I thought, "I'll be mighty, just wait for my bend."
The wind had a chuckle, I tried not to pout,
But off I decided to wiggle about!

A worm with a top hat gave me advice:
"Be silly, be scrumptious, just roll the dice."
So I strutted my stuff, in a crooked parade,
With ants at my side, sweet tunes they played!

I reached for the sun, but tripped on a stone,
"Ho ho!" laughed a crow, "Don't you moan!"
I wobbled and bounced, oh what a sight,
A dance full of giggles under each light!

Through puddles and puddles, I kept moving on,
With the rain as my partner, and weight of a fawn.
Here's to the journey, oh what a dream,
A stem with ambition, forever will beam!

Roots' Lullaby Under the Stars

Beneath the soft soil where secrets abide,
Roots gather for stories, they giggle and slide.
"Did you hear about Fern who wore a fine hat?
And danced with the raccoons? Imagine that!"

The earth made a sofa, they settled in tight,
Bouncing with laughter, a whimsical sight.
Stars peeked above, rolling their eyes,
While crickets chirped tunes, oh what a surprise!

"Once I stretched too far, into the neighbor's yard,"
Said a rooty old fellow, looking quite charred.
"They chased me with shovels and rakes all around,
I found out the hard way, keep your feet on the ground!"

So lullabies weave 'neath the blanket of night,
With roots that are dreaming, all cozy and bright.
Each chuckle, a spark, beneath twinkling light,
In a world full of giggles, everything's right!

Ballads of Blossoming Dreams

In a tiny seed a dream does brew,
A dance of roots in morning dew.
With leaves so bright, they wiggle and sway,
Even the bugs stop to laugh and play.

With sunlight's kiss and soil's delight,
They hum a tune till the fall of night.
Each petal's giggle, the breeze's tune,
A leaf ballet 'neath a cheeky moon.

Oh, how they stretch, with arms so wide,
A twirling dash in nature's stride.
They whisper secrets to the sky above,
While waving 'hello' to the clouds they love.

In this leafy land, where laughter grows,
The jester roots tickle, everybody knows.
With each tickle, the flowers cheer,
For laughter echoes, it's always near.

The Rhythm of Wooded Whispers

Hear the chatter of the branches high,
As squirrels twirl and the birds fly by.
With every breeze, the stories unfold,
Of mischievous boughs and a bark—so bold.

The wise old tree tells jokes so sweet,
About the gardeners who danced on their feet.
The flowers laugh till the petals fall,
Their giggles bouncing against each call.

The roots beneath wiggle in delight,
Spinning tales in the soft moonlight.
While shadows stretch in a playful way,
Echoing laughter that brightens the day.

Beneath this canopy, joy abounds,
Where the rhythm of growth is what resounds.
Each twig a trumpet, a call to sing,
In the woodland realm of the joyful spring.

Serenades for the Young Trunk

A trunk so young and somewhat spry,
Bends with laughter, nearly touching the sky.
It sways and bends in a carefree way,
Calling the leaves for a jazzy play.

With sunshine sparkles and rain's soft kiss,
Each new sprout dances, what pure bliss!
The young trunk grins, it's tall and proud,
Singing its songs to the cheering crowd.

Worms tell jokes in the soil below,
While roots giggle at the things they know.
A trunk so funny, with quirks and charms,
Gathers its friends with open arms.

Each day a stage, each night a dream,
The world is bright with a leafy gleam.
So raise a cheer for the trunks so free,
In their dance of joy, come join the spree!

Odes to Untamed Growth

In a patch of dirt, a sprout stands tall,
Its dreams are big, it will not fall.
With roots that tickle and shoots that tease,
It bends with the wind and dances with ease.

The sun shines down, the clouds play peek,
While giggles echo in the rustling peak.
Leaves high fives with the buzzing bees,
Nature's party, all are pleased.

A little acorn dreams of flight,
While wobbling in the morning light.
With a cheeky twist, it shouts, "I'm here!"
As critters gather for a nature cheer.

In fields of green, where laughter blooms,
A tapestry of growth that simply zooms.
So hum along, let the fun be found,
In the wild, where joy does abound.

The Art of Becoming Green

A little sprout with dreams so tall,
Wishes to dance at the garden's ball.
Sunshine giggles, rain drops cheer,
"Grow up fast, no time for fear!"

With worms for friends, they giggle and wiggle,
Telling tall tales that make them giggle.
"I'm growing leaves!" they boldly boast,
While squirrels stare like they've seen a ghost.

Beneath the sky, they sing with glee,
"Watch me now, I'm one with the tree!"
When they trip on roots and fall down now,
They laugh and say, "I'm learning how!"

So here's to growth, with all its quirks,
To little greens and big, silly perks.
With every inch, there's fun to be found,
In the art of becoming, joy's all around!

Ballad of the Urban Jungle

In the city lights, a sprout turns round,
Dodging a pigeon that's pecking the ground.
"Excuse me, sir, I need some room!"
The little green guy plans to bloom.

Cars zoom by, and folks just stare,
At ferns in the cracks, growing with flair.
"Did you see that? A leaf just waved!"
The urban jungle feels well-behaved.

The asphalt's hot, but hearts are cool,
As daisies dance through a concrete pool.
"Plant some fun where the tall tales grow,"
And watch the skyline put on a show.

With buskers playing, they sway and cheer,
The laughter of buds brings in the year.
In this bustling place, green laughs abound,
Oh, the highs and lows of a leafy crown!

Breezes Over Baby Boughs

Breezes blow softly, whisper now,
Telling tales to the leaves and how.
"Hey little buddy, stretch up high!"
The trees all giggle and wave goodbye.

A tiny branch swings, feeling free,
"I'm destined for heights, just wait and see!"
With each giggle, they sway and frolic,
Embracing the world, a little symbolic.

Birds join in with a chirpy song,
In this light-hearted realm where they belong.
"Let's have a party; bring all your friends!"
The branches twirl as the fun never ends.

So here they dance, both silly and bright,
In the sunlight's glow, they're a joyful sight.
With breezes tickling, a breeze of mirth,
Baby boughs laugh, embracing their worth!

Threads of Life's Early Tapestry

Stitching green dreams with the finest thread,
Near the roots where the giggles spread.
"I'm a fabric of fun, can't you see?"
With each tiny leaf, a new tapestry.

Woven in sunshine, laughter's embrace,
Sprouts huddle close in their happy place.
"Don't unravel now, we're just getting started!"
With tiny green hearts, they feel big-hearted.

Needles of raindrops sew a soft tune,
As butterflies dance under the moon.
"Quick, tell a joke! Make the flowers laugh!"
And everyone joins in this silly craft.

So here's the tale of life's gentle knit,
Of roots and shoots, where all joys quit.
In the early days, when life's so spry,
They weave a story that soars through the sky!

The Dance of Young Shoots

In the breeze, they twirl and bend,
Little green sprouts, they love to pretend.
Doing the jig with their roots in a knot,
Swaying to rhythms that tickle the spot.

With the sun on their leaves, they wiggle and shake,
Each tiny leaf knows just how to break.
A conga line forms, they shuffle with glee,
Oh, how they laugh at the old sturdy tree!

Some do the cha-cha, some do a slide,
While worms in the soil watch, eyes open wide.
One tells a joke, and they all seek a hug,
A party of plants, every root has a plug!

When the raindrops come, they jump and they splash,
Giggling with joy, they make quite a clash.
Who knew the green could have so much fun?
Just wait till their dance is outshone by the sun!

Dreaming in the Shade

Under broad canopies, the young ones lay,
Whispering secrets 'til the end of the day.
One little sprout dreams of cookies and cake,
While others swap tales of the breeze by the lake.

A dandelion sneezes, what a comical sight!
While little weeds giggle, all wild with delight.
A mushroom stands up, takes a bow with finesse,
"In the shade, everybody, we'll never stress!"

They share stories of thunder that made petals quake,
And of cheeky squirrels who stole their last flake.
Beneath woven boughs, their laughter unfolds,
Dreaming of mischief that nobody knows.

As the stars sprinkle down, they giggle and sigh,
"Tomorrow we'll dance like the clouds in the sky!"
Between roots and leaves, an adventure awaits,
With dreams of the forest, it's never too late!

Verses from the Forest Floor

Tiny voices echo where the critters play,
With whispers of mischief that carry away.
Mossy companions, they dance upon logs,
Sharing their tales with the bumbles and frogs.

"Did you hear 'bout the snail, so slow and so grand?
He challenged the rabbit, but won't take a stand!"
Laughter erupts from the petals nearby,
As fairies bring pixie dust with a sigh.

The ants plan a banquet, the beetles all cheer,
They'll feast on the crumbs that fall through each year.
"More cake!" the mushrooms shout, but they nibble instead,
For the frosting is sweet, dreams of sugar spread.

Among roots and leaves, funny verses align,
Each story a blossom, a twist in the vine.
So gather together, with laughter to share,
For on the forest floor, there's magic in air.

Notes of the Awakening Earth

As spring takes a bow, and the buds find their toes,
The ground's playing music as laughter bestows.
"Kick up your heels!" shouts a lively old sprout,
"Let's rock the garden, it's time to break out!"

The birds all convene for a giggle parade,
While crickets compose, serenading the glade.
A dance-off erupts with a swoop and a twirl,
As ladybugs waltz with each bright, blushing girl.

"Look at the trees!" cries a bold little sprig,
"As they shimmy and shake, isn't nature so big?"
With roots interlaced, they throw a grand bash,
A carnival of giggles, in shades, nothing brash.

With every new bloom, fresh notes fill the air,
The earth taps its rhythm, a joyful affair.
So let's sing along with a hoot and a cheer,
For life in this garden is nothing but dear!

The Story of Roots Reaching Deep

In the garden, roots did cheer,
A dance underground, oh so clear.
They whispered jokes to the worms so bright,
Beneath the soil, they laughed all night.

One root tried to tickle a stone,
But the stone just grumbled and moaned.
Another danced with a sneaky bug,
Said, "You'll only get me a snug!"

The pot they claimed as their fun spot,
A tangled mess that they forgot.
Yet every twist brought giggles true,
Roots know the best ways to pursue!

In the dirt, they made their pact,
To fun and laughter, they were hacked.
With every leaf that sways and bends,
Their whispered secrets shall not end.

Verses of Life's Silent Eruption

A seed was bored, tucked in the dirt,
Thought of a joke, and gave a spurt.
It laughed so loud, it cracked the shell,
And out it popped with a funny yell!

A sprout stretched high to catch the sun,
But slipped on dew, oh what a run!
It rolled and tumbled, roots all askew,
Shouted, "Wow! Who knew I could do that too?"

The breeze joined in, a giggling friend,
Pushed the sapling to twist and bend.
With every wiggle, a chuckle found,
Nature's comedy, all around!

As blossoms bloomed with colors bright,
They laughed at clouds, what a funny sight.
In life's garden, joy erupts, you see,
A riot of laughs, wild and free!

A Tapestry of Verdant Harmonies

In forests lush, the leaves do play,
Strumming rhymes throughout the day.
Branches shake with a merry song,
"Join us, join us, come along!"

Acorns giggle, dropped with flair,
Each tumble's met with a bold dare.
"Sway to the rhythm, let's spin and glide!
Nature's chuckles, our joy and pride!"

The bushes mumble their secret trends,
As flowers wink at their leafy friends,
Creating a tapestry, bright and loud,
Colorful laughter, they all avowed!

So if you wander through this realm,
Expect some giggles, take the helm.
In verdant tones, the joy prevails,
With nature's humor, laughter sails!

The Song of the Silent Sprout

A sprout peeked out with a funny grin,
Saw the sun, thought, "I could win!"
With tiny leaves, it waved hello,
"Come dance, dear friend, don't be so slow!"

The raindrops tittered as they fell,
Tickling petals, a joyous swell.
"Let's have a party, come join our spree,
Nature's disco under the tree!"

Each blade of grass swayed to the beat,
In the chorus of life, they found their seat.
Every gust of wind a playful tease,
Whispered jokes with gentle ease.

At dusk they sang a silly tune,
Beneath the watchful, blinking moon.
In every sprout, there's laughter true,
Join the melody, it's waiting for you!

The Gatherings of Young Pioneers

In a field of dreams they play,
Tiny tots in grand display.
With capes made of leaves and bark,
They plot adventures till it's dark.

Laughter rings through the tall grass,
Chasing bugs as moments pass.
A twig becomes a mighty sword,
Imagination's sweet reward.

They dance as shadows stretch and blend,
With roots as pals, they laugh and bend.
The mud pies served are quite the treat,
As nature joins their merry beat.

Oh, the mischief they create,
Wlth every giggle, they just can't wait.
To climb up high and shout with glee,
In a world that's wild and free.

Poetry of Roots and Raindrops

Roots whisper tales beneath our feet,
Hearing dreams of plants so sweet.
Raindrops tap with playful cheer,
Telling secrets for all to hear.

A worm winks from below ground,
As puddles form, we all jump 'round.
Laughter echoes from every side,
With soggy shoes, we take our stride.

Each dribble splash becomes a rhyme,
In this dance, we lose all time.
Giggling trees sway to the sound,
As nature's joy is all around.

These verses share our gleeful plight,
With muddy hands, we hold on tight.
In every squirt of water's flight,
We find our fun, oh what a sight!

The Awakening Chants of Greenery

In the morning light, buds arise,
Stretching limbs toward sunny skies.
Little critters sing their tune,
As flowers open, still by noon.

Squirrels bounce in playful haste,
Planting seeds without a waste.
The ants march forth, a marching band,
In nature's show, they take a stand.

Whispers of leaves tickle the breeze,
As dandelions shake with ease.
With every gust, the giggles soar,
In this garden, there's always more.

The sun beams bright, the colors sing,
With every petal, joy they bring.
In harmony they flourish, play,
In this green world, they find their way.

Chronicles from the Heart of Sap

In golden streams of sticky cheer,
The saplings laugh, their dreams so clear.
With syrup hugs and sweet delight,
They revel in the warm, bright light.

A beetle's hat, adorned with flair,
Is sported by a bug without a care.
Beneath the trunks, tales unwind,
Of playful winds and what they find.

Chasing shadows, they swing about,
In playful games that leave no doubt.
Each droplet tells a story bright,
Of friendships forged in pure daylight.

Oh, how they bicker, tease, and jest,
In every tale, they give their best.
In sap's embrace, their laughter beams,
Together weaving all their dreams.

The Cadence of Green Tendrils

In the garden, where sprouts do twist,
A tiny bean once did insist,
It stretched its leaves with flair and glee,
Said, "Look at me, I'm tall as a tree!"

The radish rolled, what a sight!
Wiggles and giggles, oh so bright,
"I'll be the star of this veggie show,
With my roots a-dancin' down below!"

A wise old pumpkin burst out in cheer,
"Who's got the best jokes? Oh my dear!"
The cabbage chimed in, "I've got a pun,
Why did the garden have so much fun?"

Now every shoot knows its own sweet song,
And plants all around just hum along,
In this patch where laughter's pure delight,
Green tendrils dance beneath the sunlight.

Breathtaking Stanzas of the Orchard

In an orchard where apples take flight,
A dapper old tree held his bark quite tight,
He whispered to pears, "Join in my spree,
We'll write a tale of fruit and glee!"

A squirrel named Nutty danced around,
With acorns aplenty, he leapt from the ground,
"I'm the author of this wild affair,
Watch as I juggle—size doesn't scare!"

Cherries chuckled in ripe, rosy glee,
"Who knew that tree would be so funny?"
While berries blushed in splendid hues,
"Let's scribble stories, what's our muse?"

So the orchard thrived in humor and cheer,
Each stem and leaf sang praises clear,
About a place of laughter and jest,
Where every fruit felt truly blessed.

The Flourishing Melody of Spring

In the springtime breeze, the flowers sway,
They gossip softly in a flowery way,
A daisy said, "Oh, did you see?
The tulip wore a hat—how fancy can it be?"

Bouncing buds joined in the fun,
"Tag, you're it! Let's all run!"
With petals flapping in joyful spins,
A symphony of laughter as the day begins.

A bee buzzed by, with jokes in tow,
"Why did the flower never play in the snow?
Because every winter, it lost its zest!
Now I'm here to make them all jest!"

So springtime danced, a canvas bright,
Painting the world in colors light,
Every bud hummed a cheerful tune,
As laughter sprouted beneath the moon.

Echoes of the Nurtured Earth

In the heart of the soil, the creatures convene,
Worms in tuxedos ready with a routine,
Said one, "Why dance underground like a fool?
Let's throw a party, let's break every rule!"

The moles popped up to catch the beat,
With shadows and giggles, they shuffled their feet,
"We're the underground kings, don't you see?
We'll dance in the dark, just you wait for me!"

A rabbit hopped in with a carrot surprise,
"This vegetable bash scores tons of highs!
Why don't we jest and tickle the roots?
Make the trees laugh with our silly hoots!"

So the earth echoed with jubilant mirth,
A celebration of life, of nurturing birth,
Where every critter joined in delight,
In the rich, dark soil, everything felt right.

The Call and Response of Nature's Essence

Hey there, little sprout, what do you see?
A busy bumblebee, buzzing close to me!
Do you hear their dance? It's quite a sight!
They think I'm a flower, but I'm not that bright!

Look up to the sky, what's that you feel?
A raindrop just plopped, like nature's meal!
It tickles my leaves, oh what a prank!
I guess I'll just grow, in this muddy bank!

The sun's shining down, with a cheeky grin,
Saying, "Grow up tall, let the fun begin!"
But watch out for birds, they're plotting a feast,
I might need a hat, or I'll be their least!

So here I stand, with roots sunk deep,
Life's a funny game, and I'm diving deep!
With giggles and wiggles, oh what a scene,
I'm the jester of the garden, clad in green!

Verses from the Garden's Heart

In the garden bed, there's quite a show,
Plants gossiping softly, 'Did you see that crow?'
He swoops and he dives, just looking for snacks,
It's hard to be brave when you're facing such hacks!

The carrots protest, "We're too cute to eat!"
While onions just laugh, "We're smelling so sweet!"
"Don't cry, dear cucumbers," I said with a cheer,
"Let's dress up in dill, then we've nothing to fear!"

The lettuce is bending, getting all fluffed,
Saying, "I'm too crisp, it's getting real tough!"
While the radishes snicker from down in the dirt,
"Just wait for the salad, we'll see who gets hurt!"

Together we giggle, in bright sunny rays,
Playing our roles in nature's mad plays!
So here's to the garden, a whimsical place,
Where laughter and growing have a funny face!

Reflections of Growth in Stillness

In a quiet patch, where the shadows creep,
Tiny faces peek, from their earthy sleep!
"Are you awake?" whispers a bold little sprig,
"Just stretching my leaves, I'm no sleepy pig!"

A snail slides by, with an air of great flair,
He's taking his time, no rush anywhere!
"Hey buddy, let's race," shouts a spunky old toad,
"Just hop on my back, let's share this slow road!"

The mushrooms are chuckling, all plump and round,
"Mushrooming's tough when you're stuck in the ground!"

Yet they sprout out loud, with colors so bold,
Painting the earth in crimson and gold!

So here's to our stillness, to moments we share,
Where roots intertwine and hang in mid-air.
Nature's a jester, a trickster so grand,
In her quiet reflections, we all understand!

The Celebration of Green Surge

Oh, the thrill of spring is bursting with zeal,
Every leaf has a story, a dance, a squeal!
The daisies are twirling, dressed in their best,
While dandelions giggle at every new jest!

The violets are chatting, their colors ablaze,
"Let's throw a party, let's lighten the haze!"
But oh dear, the weeds, they want to join too,
"Don't pull us, we promise to bring something new!"

The sun throws confetti, all golden and bright,
While the clouds puff up, ready for a flight!
Together we frolic, with laughter and cheers,
Celebrating the blooms, through all of our years!

So here's to the green surge, a riotous shout,
With joy and some mischief, we swap all about!
From roots to the tips, let the fun resonate,
In this garden of giggles, oh isn't it great?

Tuning into Fresh Horizons

A little sprout with a funny hat,
Dancing around like a curious cat.
Waving its leaves in the morning sun,
Whispering secrets, oh what fun!

Squirrels can't help but stop and stare,
At the tiny tree doing its hair.
With roots that giggle and branches that sway,
It's the quirkiest show, come see the play!

It's growing tall with a cheeky grin,
Like a jester joined in the garden din.
Each day brings laughter, a new surprise,
Who knew plants had such funny highs?

To fresh horizons, this plant will drive,
With a twirl and a whirl, it comes alive.
In soil it casts its silly spell,
Tuning in where the giggles dwell!

The Blooms' Silent Symphony

In the garden's heart, a bloom does hum,
Playing notes like a thumping drum.
Petals clapping, leaves taking flight,
Under stars, they dance through the night.

A flower's laughter, soft and sweet,
Bees join in with their buzzing beat.
The daisies giggle, the roses wink,
In this silent jam, all plants link!

A dance-off blooms, the tulips prance,
Spinning around in a wild romance.
The sunflowers laugh, oh what a sight,
In this symphony built of pure delight.

The breeze plays softly, a teasing wind,
As the blooms bow down, their show to end.
With a nod and a tip, they take their leave,
In the silent symphony, we all believe!

Embrace of the First Light

Morning unfolds with a twinkling grin,
As little plants wake and stretch within.
Sunbeams peek through the leaves so spry,
  Giving the garden a bright, funny high!

The daffodils giggle, their petals ablaze,
  Finding joy in the new sun's rays.
With a wink to the world, they sway and bow,
  Embracing the light, in the here and now.

  The cacti pose with a tough little dance,
  While ferns do flips, oh what a chance!
  Every blossom makes a comic show,
  In this first light, they steal the glow!

With laughter and shine, they greet the morn,
  In the embrace of the light, we are reborn.
    Life's a joke, just wait and see,
    In this garden glee, we all agree!

Rhythms of Emerging Growth

New sprouts are jigging, oh what a scene,
In the rhythm of life, they dance so keen.
Roots like maracas, shaking with cheer,
As nature's concert draws all near.

The thyme's doing salsa, basil a twist,
Each little leaf joins in, none are missed.
Pumpkins are rolling, quite out of beat,
But the laughter they bring is oh-so-sweet!

The grasshoppers hop, adding to the mix,
While the ants form a line for more funny tricks.
With every new bud, the laughter grows,
A comedic chorus, as everyone knows.

In this dance of life, there's joy to find,
With rhythms of growth, it's all intertwined.
As nature giggles, together we sway,
In this quirky garden, come join the play!

Harmonies of Fresh Leaves

A leaf sneezed, oh what a sound,
The other trees gathered 'round.
"Bless you!" they chimed, in delight,
As the wind giggled, taking flight.

Branches swayed in silly dances,
While roots shared their best prances.
Buds whispered jokes, sweet and spry,
While nearby bees buzzed with a sigh.

A squirrel dropped its acorn stash,
It rolled past, oh what a crash!
The laughter sprouted in the air,
As critters joined the joyful affair.

So, revel in this leafy tune,
Underneath the bright, full moon.
For every rustle sings along,
In the forest's merry song.

Lullabies of the Early Sprout

There once was a sprout, quite shy and small,
It wore a cap made of dew, after all.
It sang to the worms, in whispers so sweet,
While ants danced around on their tiny, bare feet.

The ladybugs clapped, their spots all a-twirl,
As the sprout shared tales of its dreams to unfurl.
The soil chuckled softly, quite deep and profound,
As the sprout made new friends from the ground all around.

A caterpillar joined, with a wiggle and twist,
Said, "Join in my band, you must not be missed!"
With a leaf for a drum and a twig for a flute,
The early sprout grooved, oh what a hoot!

So sing to the stars when night starts to fall,
For even the sprout has a dream to enthrall.
Let lullabies cradle the night's gentle air,
As the laughter of nature ignites everywhere.

Chirping Around the Young Tree

In the shade of a tree, the birds hold a feast,
A chirping brigade, from the greatest to least.
"Who stole my worm?" cried a bright little lark,
As the worms all giggled, tucked under the bark.

A squirrel, quite proud, wore a nut for a hat,
While a rabbit rolled by on a skateboard, imagine that!
The tree chuckled deep, feeling all kinds of glee,
As the critters held court, oh what a ruckus, you see!

"Jump higher! Flap faster!" the bluejay would rail,
While the magpie brought gossip, not one piece stale.
With a flurry of feathers, they sang through the day,
Under the branches where the children would play.

So listen intently, let your worries just flee,
For laughter and chirps are the sound of the free.
Around the young tree, let fun never cease,
In this playful symphony, we find our release.

Celebrations of the Seedling

A seedling decided to throw a grand show,
Inviting the critters, both high and below.
With sunlight as stage light, and dirt as the ground,
The laughter exploding, oh what joy abound!

The beetles brought snacks, in a leaf-toting line,
While butterflies twirled, perfect and fine.
"It's a party!" they chirped, "Come join in the fun!"
With the roots in a jig, and the branches that run.

A firefly flicked lights, like stars on the floor,
While the grasshoppers leaped, claiming they wanted more.
The excitement kept growing, as night turned to day,
In the heart of the garden, where the critters would play.

So gather around, let the festivities ring,
For even a seedling can dance and can sing.
In the laughter of nature, we all feel alive,
In these jubilant gatherings, sweet joy will thrive.

The Language of Sprouting Life

In the garden, seedlings speak,
Whispering secrets, oh so meek.
They giggle as they stretch and sway,
Who knew plants could laugh all day?

Worms rumble with a wiggly tune,
Under the sun, they dance at noon.
Flowers chuckle, petals all a-flutter,
While lazy bees just buzz and mutter.

A grapevine grins, with juicy cheer,
Saying 'Wine not? Come have a beer!'
The snap peas snap with witty jest,
They joke that they are simply the best.

Oh, the chives in their funny hats,
Laughing at the garden's clever chats.
Nature's banter, a comic spree,
In the soil, we're all plant-free!

Serenade of the Sap

In the trees, a sticky tune,
Sap sings sweetly, morning to noon.
It drips and drops in a funny way,
Sticky fingers, what a day!

Bumblebees buzz with silly glee,
Dancing 'round the old oak tree.
The squirrels chuckle at their flight,
While acorns fall with soft delight.

A wise old owl sings out of turn,
"Why do trees make such a churn?"
And all the critters laugh along,
In the woods, we all belong!

From every branch, a hearty laugh,
Nature's humor tells the half.
With every drop of smiling sap,
It's a world of joy, a funny map!

Where Green Dreams Begin

In the soil, where dreams commence,
Worms plot out their next defense.
Seeds are stretching, oh so spry,
'Watch us grow!' they shout, oh my!

Little sprouts with big ambitions,
Mapping out their sweet renditions.
"Is this the spot for my debut?"
A debate starts, oh, who knew?

The flowers vie for the best view,
While daisies wear a crown or two.
"Let's bloom in colors, loud and bright!"
They giggle through the starry night.

Where green dreams dance and tease the sun,
Every laugh makes growing fun.
In the field, silliness prevails,
A raucous cheer throughout the trails!

Chants of the Burgeoning Vale

In the vale, the plants convene,
A chorus of leaves—what a scene!
They sing of rain and sunshine rays,
While critters join in funny plays.

The daisies wear their whitest dress,
Complaining of the bugs, no less.
"What's that tickle?" they giggle and twirl,
"Oh dear me, is it a whirligig girl?"

A dandelion shouts with glee,
"Blow me away, come set me free!"
While the rushes sway side to side,
Finding humor is their pride.

In the vale where laughter reigns,
Each gust of wind brings joyful strains.
With every bloom there's a hearty cheer,
In nature's song, we've nothing to fear!

Cadence of the Forest's Youth

In a forest where giggles sprout,
Tiny trees form a cheerful shout.
With leaves that wiggle in the sun,
They dance around, oh what fun!

Squirrels jest as branches sway,
Telling jokes in a bushy way.
A rabbit hops, a deer sings,
While fluttering birds share gossip springs.

Sunbeams tickle the playful boughs,
Each one chuckling, taking bows.
The roots below form a silly band,
As nature plays, they all understand.

In this grove of laughter and cheer,
Every twig whispers, "Life's a beer!"
So join the symphony, let it erupt,
For in this youth, all joy's corrupt!

Songs in the Soft Earth

Beneath the soil, a chorus hums,
Where worms gyrate and dig their drums.
With rhythm of burrows, they sway side to side,
Planting tickles where roots abide.

Moles form a band with their shovels so bright,
Playing tunes in the cool moonlight.
Ants rush around on an endless quest,
Traffic chaos, their tiny fest!

The daisies gossip as they poke their heads,
"Who's the silliest among the beds?"
Laughter echoes as blossoms bloom,
In this merry dance, there's always room.

So let's celebrate the whispers down low,
Where nature's antics always steal the show!
And every seed keeping time in the dirt,
Turns to songs as the world feels flirt.

Whistles of the Woodland Spring

In the woods, where laughter swells,
A whistling breeze shares its silly spells.
Trees crack up when the brook slides by,
While frogs leap high and croak "Oh my!"

Budding branches wear hats made of dew,
They strut like fashionistas, who knew?
With every pluck of a leaf, they jest,
In this leafy haven, they're truly blessed.

Bees buzz along, quite the chatterboxes,
Making honey and plotting their fox tricks.
A deer trips over roots, what a sight!
The woodland giggles at this pure delight.

So join this frolic in the leafy sea,
Where every rustle holds a mystery.
Let the laughter echo, let joy spring forth,
In this kingdom of whimsy, we find our worth.

Tales of Tender Growth

Once upon a time in a sprouting place,
Tiny shoots sprouted, all with a face.
They shared stories of how they'd thrive,
Laughing and dreaming to feel alive.

One said, "I'll be a tree quite tall!
But first, let's have a poppy ball!"
With petals swirling like socks in the wind,
The forest joined in, where fun would begin.

A flower snapped a selfie with a bee,
"Say cheese!" they buzzed in jubilee.
With the sun beaming down on this show,
Each sprout agreed, "We're the stars of the glow!"

So gather the seeds, spread joy all around,
For every little sprout knows laughter is found.
In a world of wonders where friendships grow,
They'll always have tales to tell as they glow.

Nature's Breath of New Beginnings

Tiny leaves poke through soil,
To greet the sun, they toil.
A squirrel glances, twitching its tail,
Laughing at the sprout's first fail.

Worms wiggle in a game of chase,
As raindrops tickle each green face.
The breeze whispers with a jest,
Nature's way of being blessed.

Each bud is like a hopeful grin,
Shouting, 'Let the fun begin!'
Pollen dances like a clown,
In this thriving, leafy town.

Roots dig deep, they take a stand,
Grasping tightly with tender hand.
As birds chirp silly little tunes,
The earth hums laughter to the moons.

The Dance of Emerging Foliage

Watch them sway, a leafy show,
In rhythm with the breeze they go.
Twigs wiggle, making merry sounds,
Nature's dance spins all around.

Each little bud, a tiny jive,
Their joyful moves keep them alive.
A deer joins in with an awkward prance,
In the forest's wild dance romance.

Grass blades giggle in sunny light,
As daisies bloom, oh what a sight!
A butterfly flutters, donning a hat,
Joining the fun, imagine that!

Clouds drift by, they float and tease,
As flowers sway with charming ease.
Together they laugh, nature's delight,
In this grand show of pure sunlight.

Voices of the Growing Grove

In the grove, the trees debate,
Who can stretch the tallest straight?
A crow quips from a bough so high,
"Just look at us, we could touch the sky!"

Beneath the shade, the critters meet,
Sharing tales of summer heat.
"Do you think it's time to grow?"
"Not yet!" the mushrooms say, "Not so!"

A rabbit hops, its ears so wide,
Eavesdropping on the leafy pride.
"Hey, who invited that old oak?"
"Let's ask him, I heard him joke!"

With whispers soft, the leaves exchange,
Stories of dreams and funny change.
Together they sing, a sweet refrain,
In harmony with the soft, warm rain.

Chants of the Shaded Path

On the path where shadows play,
Whispers buzz, the trees convey.
"Hey, did you hear the last big joke?"
"It cracked me up, that funny oak!"

Twisting vines, they weave a tale,
Of picnic ants using a pail.
"Do you think they'll bring the snacks?"
"Only if they avoid the tracks!"

Sunbeams sneak in for a peek,
Laughter lingers though they're meek.
The flowers giggle, what a scene,
As butterflies glide, so serene.

Nature's chorus, full of cheer,
Echos of joy all around here.
On this path, where fun is rife,
The trees all dance, embracing life.

The Soliloquy of Nature's Youth

In a garden of sprout, where mischief abounds,
A young tree told secrets to squirrels and hounds.
"I stretch for the sky, like a cat on a beam,
But my roots are still pulling, I'm stuck in a dream!"

With whispers of wind, the leaves started to giggle,
"You think you're so tall, but you still need a wiggle!"
The earth shook with laughter at how trees like to boast,
Yet they'd trip on their roots, making nature their host.

In the shade of the branches, the critters convene,
To plan out their pranks, and keep it all clean.
"Let's tickle the branches, give the birds quite a fright,
We'll hide in the bushes 'til the darkness takes flight!"

So with giggles and rustles, they plotted away,
The youthful exuberance turned night into day.
For in nature's backyard, where laughter is beans,
The spirit of youth is as wild as it seems!

Chronicles of the Growing Canopy

There once was a willow that wore a big frown,
It sighed to the sky, "I'm the loneliest clown!"
The oak heard the woe and said, "Don't be a bore,
I'll give you my acorns, just open the door!"

So they threw a grand party with branches entwined,
'Neath the stars they all rallied, excitement aligned.
The mushrooms brought snacks, while the ferns played the tunes,
They danced 'til the sun broke, with joy in their blooms.

With each floating feather, and each tickling breeze,
The trees swayed together, much like a big tease.
To the rhythm of nature, they each shared a song,
In the canopy crowded, where friendships grow strong!

The willow now giggles, with friends by its side,
Underneath the blue sky, they take quite a ride.
For in every good plot where the leaves find delight,
The chronicles echo, of friendships so bright!

Reflections in the Dew-Kissed Grass

A dewdrop once told, "I'm a gem of the morn!"
While the blades wore their coats, like a field of fine corn.

"Come dance with us, sunshine, don't be such a bore!"
As the butterflies giggled and asked for much more.

The grass whispered softly, full of humor and sass,
"We're the floor of the fairies! They prance on our mass!"

With a hop and a skip, the blooms joined the fun,
As the dew drops kept shining, under rays of the sun.

In the minutes that passed, a worm wiggled near,
"You think you're so fancy, but I bring the cheer!"
The daisies erupted in petals of glee,
As the world rolled along, playful as can be.

So listen to nature, for laughter fills air,
With each drop of dew, love and joy we all share.
The reflections of life, through the grass oh so fine,
Are filled with the humor, of nature's design!

Notes from the Burgeoning Bough

From the boughs of the trees, there came a loud shout,
A squirrel claimed victory, "I'll leap without doubt!"
But a branch started creaking, said, "That's quite a leap!
You might find yourself landing in a pile of heaps!"

At the edge of the limb, the laughter spread wide,
As birds chirped the tune of a wobbly ride.
"Come on little buddy, don't lose your sweet flair!
The sky's full of wonders, it's just up in the air!"

But the squirrel, undeterred, took off with a squeak,
Flipping, then flopping, it had quite the tweak!
The bough shook in laughter, while the branches all swayed,
As the critters enjoyed the pranks that they played.

So heed the wise words of the trees and the breeze,
Life's filled with adventures, just do as you please.
In the canopy high, where the giggles arise,
The notes of the boughs sing of fun in the skies!

www.ingramcontent.com/pod-product-compliance
Lightning Source LLC
Chambersburg PA
CBHW071813160426
43209CB00003B/64